THE BIG BOOK OF CENTRAL AMERICA AND THE CARIBBEAN

Geography Facts Book
Children's Geography & Culture Books

BABY PROFESSOR
EDUCATION KIDS

Speedy Publishing LLC

40 E. Main St. #1156

Newark, DE 19711

www.speedypublishing.com

Copyright 2017

Here's your instant travel pass to countries, climates, and land forms that are fascinating and beautiful. Let's go visit Central America and the Caribbean!

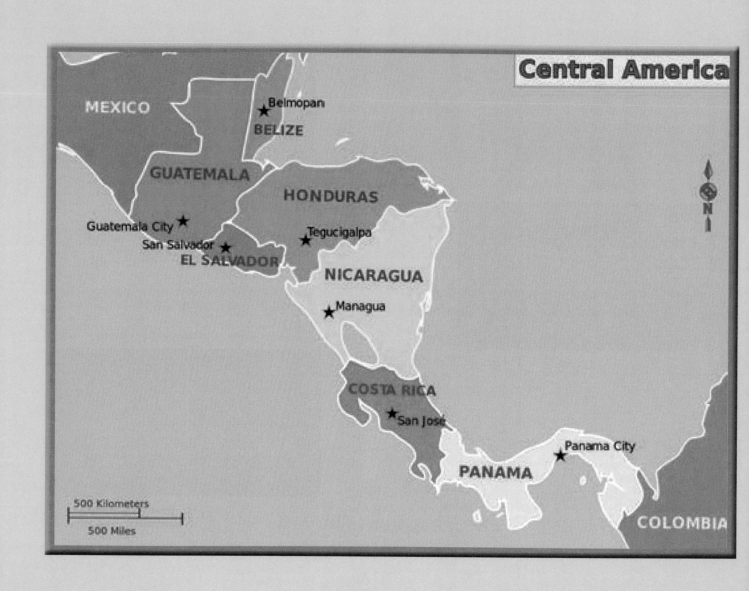

MAP OF CENTRAL AMERICA

Central America joins North and South America, and divides the Pacific Ocean from the Caribbean. Even though it is a narrow territory with no spot more than 125 miles away from the ocean, it has beauty and complexity for those who look closely.

Over 40 million people live in Central America, as citizens of seven different countries: Belize, Honduras, Guatemala, El Salvador, Nicaragua, Costa Rica, and Panama. More than half of the people are of mixed European and Mayan heritage, and about 20 percent are descendants of the tribes that lived here before the Europeans arrived. The area was thickly settled before "the conquest" by Europeans, and many of these older cultures and peoples have been lost.

A BEACH IN PANAMA

TAJUMULCO VOLCANO, GUATEMALA

The longest mountain ranges are the Cordillera de Talamance, the Sierra Madre de Chiapas, and the Cordillera Isabelia. The highest point in Central America is a 14,000-foot volcano, Tajumulco, in Guatemala. These mountains are rugged and picturesque.

Much of the population of Guatemala, Costa Rica, and Honduras lives in valleys between the mountain ranges. The valleys are fertile, and are good places to raise both animals and crops.

Along both the Atlantic and Pacific coasts are lowlands which are hotter and more humid than the drier, cooler mountains.

Many of the mountains in the region are active volcanoes, and Central America has seen several major eruptions causing destruction and death. On the other hand, many crops grow very well on rich volcanic soil, so the volcanoes also make good harvests possible.

ARENAL VOLCANO, COSTA RICA

A LAVA IN PACAYA, GUATEMALA

Many of the volcanoes, both active and dormant, are part of the Central American Volcanic Arc, or CAVA. CAVA follows Central America's Pacific coastline for almost a thousand miles, where two tectonic plates are slowly colliding. The result of the collision, over thousands of years, is volcanic activity and the impressive mountain ranges of Central America. The volcanoes range from lava domes to gigantic stratovolcanoes.

Some of the volcanoes have experienced huge eruptions, one of the most recent being in 1902. Active volcanoes include Arenal and Turrialba in Costa Rica, Nicagragua's Cerro Negro and Concepción, Izalco and San Miguel in El Salvador, and Fuego in Guatemala. Learn more about volcanoes in the Baby Professor book, What Happens Before and After Volcanoes Erupt?

IZALCO VOLCANO

RAINFOREST

In 1950, forests covered over half of Central America. The rain forests, though tiny compared to those of South America, hold a wide diversity of animal and plant species. Panama, for instance, has over 700 species of birds, more than in all of North America, which is much larger.

However, ambitious logging has reduced the forests dramatically and has put many species at risk. El Salvador, for instance, has almost no forest left at all. This affects more than just the countries in the region. Three of the four major migratory routes for birds between North and South America pass along Central America. With the loss of habitat the migrating species need, birds like the wood thrush are becoming rare in North America because they cannot complete their migration.

JUAYÚA, EL SALVADOR

FOREST IN BELIZE

Steps are under way to preserve and promote the forests, but it will take a change in the way people think about nature—that it is more than just resources to extract and use—before the trend toward stripping the region of its forests will reverse.

LAKES AND RIVERS

The largest rivers in Central America flow toward the Caribbean, but there are smaller rivers and streams that run to the Pacific Ocean. Many are too small or too steep to be used by boats, especially on the Pacific side.

Central America has only three large lakes. Nicaragua has Lake Managua and

Lake Nicaragua, while Gatun Lake in Panama has been incorporated into the Panama Canal.

GATUN LAKE

As well as good land for many crops, Central America has deposits of nickel and iron, extensive forests, and some oil. Its offshore waters are rich in fish. However, resource extraction has not been done in a sustainable way. Clearcutting of forests leads to landslides, erosion, and pollution of rivers.

Mining has also led to water pollution. Some fish species are suffering because of the heavy catches fishing fleets bring in.

PANAMA CANAL

One great asset Central America has is its location and shape. This narrow stretch of land is on a good shipping route between Asia and Europe, and a huge number of ships pass through the Panama Canal rather than travelling all the way around South America. Even before the canal was first built in the early part of the 20th century, merchants would sail to one Central American coast, use horses and mules to carry their cargo to the other coast, and use a second ship to carry the cargo toward its destination.

CLIMATE

Central America has two seasons: the hot, wet summer and the drier winter which is a bit cooler. Temperatures depend on the trade winds, which can bring cooler air as well as rain.

HURRICANE MITCH IN HONDURAS

Along with volcanic eruptions, Central America is often the landing place for hurricanes and their devastating winds. With hurricanes come floods in the lowlands; often thousands die and many thousands more lose their homes. Hurricane Mitch in 1998 hit Honduras and Nicaragua very hard.

THE CARIBBEAN

East of Central America lies the Caribbean, a sea of the Atlantic Ocean that washes the shores of over seven thousand islands. They range from large islands like Cuba, Hispaniola, Jamaica, and Puerto Rico to tiny specks that are too small to support much life. Only two percent of the islands have human populations!

A BEAUTIFUL BEACH IN THE CARRIBEAN

A TRADITIONAL PERFORMER FROM FUTUNA ISLAND

Over 43 million people live in the Caribbean, as citizens of 28 different countries plus territories of more distant countries like Britain, the Netherlands, and the United States.

GEOGRAPHY

The Caribbean islands vary widely in their geography. Some, like Aruba and Barbados, are fairly flat and have little or no volcanic action. Others were formed by volcanoes and have prominent volcanic cones in their centers. Some islands, like Cuba, Hispaniola, Puerto Rico, Saint Thomas, and Grenada, have significant mountain ranges with rugged peaks.

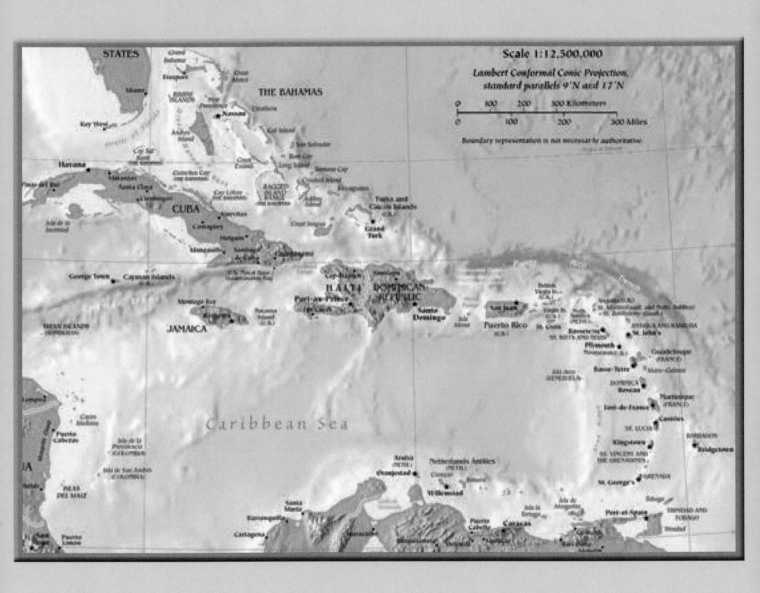

MAP OF THE CARIBBEAN

Volcanic activity is not just a pretty event on the horizon. When the Soufriere hills volcano on Montserrat became active in 1995, after giving occasional shocks every thirty years or so, the continuing eruptions have meant nobody can live on most of

SOUFRIERE HILLS

Montserrat any more. Over two thirds of the population has moved away. Evacuation of the capital, Plymouth, took place just a few weeks before an eruption and lava flow buried the city.

RIVERS AND LAKES

The islands of the Caribbean have many streams and short rivers, but few significant lakes or freshwater bodies. The longest river, in Cuba, is the Cauto, which is over 230 miles long.

CAUTO, CUBA

LAKE ENRIQUILLO

However, there is a mystery concerning two lakes. On Hispaniola, the island shared by Haiti and the Dominican Republic, two lakes are rising quickly. Lake Azuéi has submerged what was a shoreline community in Haiti. Lake Enriquillo in the Dominican Republic, the largest lake in the Caribbean, has risen over 30 feet in ten years.

The rise of the lakes has drowned farmlands, and some of the thousands of displaced farmers have turned to making charcoal to support themselves. This puts added pressure on the forests of Hispaniola.

Nobody yet has a theory as to why these lakes are rising.

HISPANIOLAN PINE FOREST

A TROPICAL ISLAND

The Caribbean ranges from tropical to subtropical. It is sunny all year round, with half the year being wetter with daily rain showers, and the other half drier. The temperature only varies a couple of degrees in any given place over the whole year in much of the Caribbean.

Warm, moist wind from the east can cause sharp divisions where the eastern side of an island hosts a rain forest and further to the west, on the other side of a mountain range, there is a near-desert.

Hurricanes are a huge and powerful part of the Caribbean experience. Most hurricanes appear in August and September, but they can start to cause havoc as early as June and as late as November.

A SATELLITE VIEW OF A HURRICANE

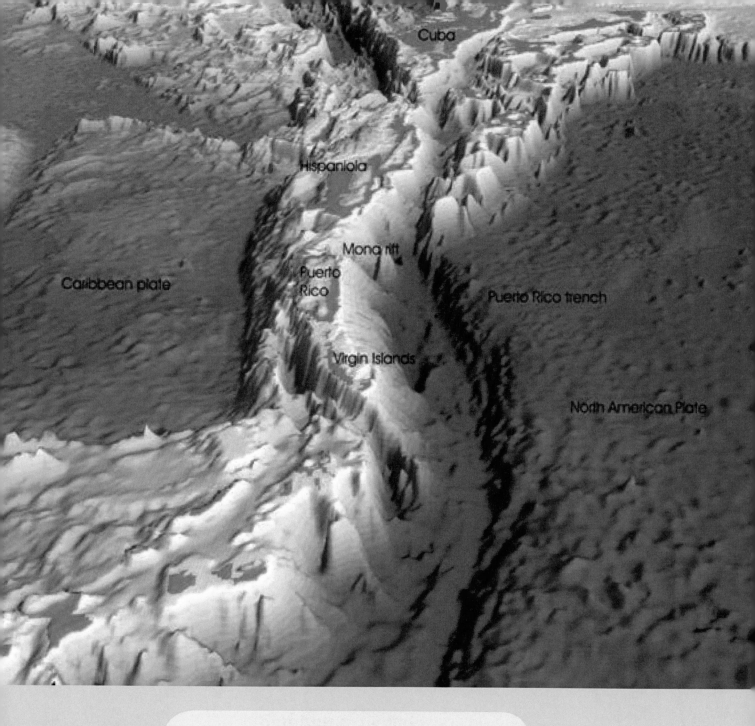

Cuba

Hispaniola

Mona rift

Puerto
Rico

Caribbean plate

Puerto Rico trench

Virgin Islands

North American Plate

ATLANTIC TRENCH

THE SEA

The deepest point of the whole Atlantic Ocean, the Puerto Rico Trench, is part of the Caribbean. The area is rich in fish, turtles, and birds of many kinds.

The Caribbean has almost ten percent of the Earth's coral reefs, covering over 20,000 square miles.

THE ISLAND GROUPS

Most of the islands in the Caribbean are part of the Greater Antilles, a chain stretching from Mexico to near Venezuela. This group includes the Bahamas, Cuba, Haiti, the Caymans, the Dominican Republic, Puerto Rico, and Jamaica.

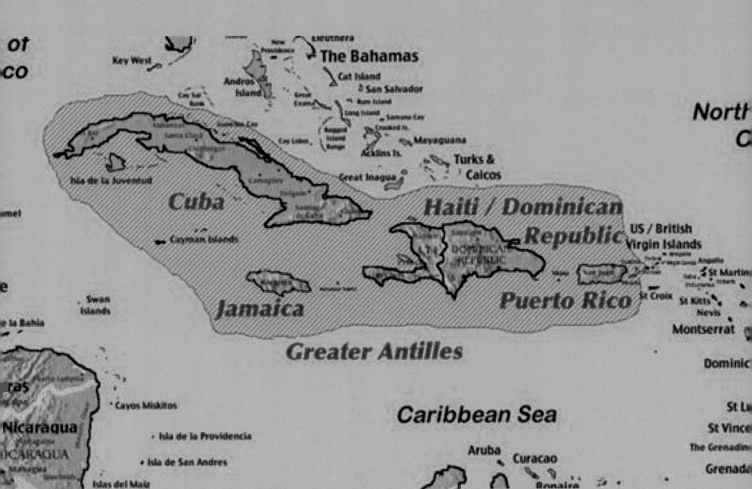

GREATER ANTILLES ISLANDS

A related chain of islands, the Lesser Antilles, includes Saint Maartin, Antigua, Saint Kitts and Nevis, Montserrat, Guadeloupe, and the U.S. and British Virgin Islands.

Aruba, Bonaire, and Curacao are part of the Leeward Islands; while Dominica, Martinique, Saint Lucia, Saint Vincent and the Grenadines, Grenada, Barbados, and Trinidad and Tobago are in the Windward Islands.

LEARN MORE ABOUT OUR EARTH

Central America connects North and South America, and often is considered part of North America. Read the Baby Professor book, North America: The Third Largest Continent, to learn about the big neighbor of Central America and the Caribbean.

Visit

BABY PROFESSOR

www.BabyProfessorBooks.com

to download Free Baby Professor eBooks
and view our catalog of new and exciting
Children's Books

Made in the USA
Lexington, KY
03 December 2018